AFTER DINNER

Andrew Bovell

CURRENCY PRESS
SYDNEY

CURRENCY PLAYS

First published in 1989
by Currency Press Pty Ltd,
PO Box 2287, Strawberry Hills, NSW, 2012, Australia
enquiries@currency.com.au
www.currency.com.au

Copyright © Andrew Bovell, 1988, 1997
Revised edition published in 1997
This edition published in 2012
Reprinted 2012, 2019.

NATIONAL LIBRARY OF AUSTRALIA CIP DATA

Author: Bovel, Andrew.
Title: After dinner / Andrew Bovell.
ISBN: 9780868195186 (pbk.)
Dewey Number: A822.3

Typeset by Emily Ralph for Currency Press.
Cover design by Lisa White for Currency Press.

Contents

Author's Note   v

AFTER DINNER

   Act One   1

   Act Two   45

Currency Press acknowledges the Traditional Owners of the Country on which we live and work. We pay our respects to all Aboriginal and Torres Strait Islander Elders, past and present.

Author's Note

Andrew Bovell

I wrote this play ten years ago. I never thought it would last this long. I imagined it would be one of those plays that comes on at La Mama, lasts for three weeks and is never heard of again. In fact that initial season lasted for fifteen weeks, after transferring from La Mama to Theatre Works in St Kilda and then to the Universal in Fitzroy. By the time it was winding up in Melbourne three interstate companies were applying for the rights, including the Griffin Theatre Company in Sydney. Since then there's been over twenty professional productions of the play, including one in London and one in Dublin. And now, in 1997, the Melbourne Theatre Company and Black Swan in Perth are both undertaking productions.

After Dinner has just kept on keeping on, defying those early expectations of its author. It holds a special place among the plays and screenplays I have written because every time I've been broke and about to give the business of writing away a royalties cheque has arrived, as if to tell me not to give up. The cheques are rarely substantial but they have proved to be priceless in terms of boosting a writer's morale.

With the MTC's upcoming production and a new Currency Press publication of the text I've had the opportunity to consider the play once again and to think about its history.

I usually find it difficult to identify the genesis of a play. That's not the case with *After Dinner*. It was a moment glimpsed at the Tankerville Arms in Fitzroy in 1984. Three women were sitting at a table in the empty bistro arguing about how to divide the bill. One woman in particular was insistent that it should be done fairly. She seemed so concerned that she would have to pay more than her share. It was an excruciating moment, mundane and quintessentially Australian.

It wasn't the comedy of the situation that immediately struck me. It was its pathos. It said something to me about loneliness and the absence of love, about being stuck in a place and not knowing how to move forward, about coming up against your own limitations, about being furious with life and what it has failed to provide. It was probably a lot to read into such a simple moment. The woman concerned was probably just being careful with her money. But that's a playwright for you.

I got home that night and wrote. Dympie, Monika and Paula were born onto the page with surprising ease. This material formed the basis of a short play called *Dinner and Then Entertainment*. This was a Beckett like piece about three women stuck in a restaurant, consumed by fantasies of the exotic while being trapped in the banal. I was studying at the Victorian College of the Arts at the time. It was the end of our first semester and I workshopped the play with fellow students, Suzanne Kersten, Eugenia Fragos, Angela Seaward and Suzanne Shaw.

We presented it to the rest of the Drama School and received an amazing response. The piece had struck a chord. It was the first time I experienced the rush of adrenalin a writer gets when a magical connection occurs between a performance and its audience. If I had any doubts about what I wanted to be, it was that moment that dispelled them.

In 1986 I revived the piece for our graduation day performance. In this incarnation it became a comic sketch about three very ordinary women trying their hardest to have a good time when everything that could go wrong did. Eugenia played Paula again and was joined this time by Kim Trengove as Dympie and Mary Lou (Cabbage) Thorpe as Monika. It received an enthusiastic response from a demanding audience of industry heavyweights. It was a great feeling watching a theatre full of agents and artistic directors laugh their heads off. I can remember being surprised that something I had written could make people laugh like that. I had always regarded myself as a fairly serious young writer and my work more akin to the tragic side of life. I guess the lesson was that the line between tragedy and comedy is very thin and *After Dinner* managed to walk it.

I finally got around to writing the full length version of the play towards the end of 1987. It wasn't until this stage that Gordon and

Stephen were created. I wrote it quickly in a mad rush, allowing the natural structure of an evening out to emerge and guide the play. Some critics have said that it's unevenly structured and raw in its conception. Others have said that its structure and the rhythm of movement of action between the tables is perfectly judged. I don't know any more. What I do know is that it was one of those writing experiences where the characters just took off and led the action.

I wrote it specifically for Kim Durban to direct and for five friends who were all unemployed actors at the time. Eugenia re-invented Paula for the third time, Kim Trengove played Dympie again and they were joined by Leigh Morgan playing Monika. Tom Gutteridge took on Gordon and Peter Murphy played Stephen.

I owe a great deal to Kim and this fantastic group of actors. It was a new play and the style was initially unclear. It's not an easy piece to get right. If the comedy is played too hard then it can seem judgmental of the characters. But if the pain and loneliness of the characters is played too close to the surface at the expense of the humour then the audience is prevented from fully empathising with the characters. Without the humour it's difficult to identify with them.

The fact that the play has had such an extended life is in part due to the initial production managing the balance between humour and pathos so well. They showed others that it could work and gave me the confidence to believe that I could write.

Like me they never expected to be stuck with these characters for so long. For a while the actors felt like the characters had taken over. Tom confesses that it took several years for him to rid himself of Gordon and he still finds himself occasionally lapsing into Gordon's terrible insecurities. Likewise Kim finds herself curling her lip with disapproval just like Dympie and I still find Eugenia occasionally dancing in a world all of her own just like Paula.

Similarly, I owe my thanks to Currency Press. Currency initially published the play as part of their Current Theatre Series, in conjunction with Ian Watson's production at Griffin in 1989. We can't underestimate the importance of published works. It allows plays to be accessible and means that they are documented and distributed way beyond the reach of word of mouth or good reviews. I can only hope that this new edition sees the play through another ten years.

After Dinner was first performed at La Mama, Melbourne, 20 April 1988 with the following cast:

GORDON	Tom Gutteridge
DYMPIE	Kim Trengove
PAULA	Eugenia Fragos
MONIKA	Leigh Morgan
STEPHEN	Peter Murphy

Director, Kim Durban
Designer, Amanda Johnson
Stage Manager, Jane Allen
Music, Tom Gillick and The Heartbreaks

CHARACTERS

GORDON, a bank worker, mid-thirties.
DYMPIE, an office worker, mid-thirties.
PAULA, an office worker, mid-thirties.
MONIKA, an office worker, mid-thirties.
STEPHEN, a bank worker, mid-thirties.

SETTING

The action takes place on a Friday evening at a suburban pub/bistro.

ACT ONE

A suburban pub-bistro. The reserved area for meals, around seven p.m. on a Friday evening. The focus of the room is on two separate tables, each set for three. On each there is a burning candle, plastic covered menus, a small vase with three wilted flowers and an ashtray. Elsewhere is the bar, the dance floor, the dance platform and the toilets.

GORDON sits alone at one of the tables. He has been there for some time. He checks his watch then goes to have a drink. His glass is empty, so he tries to catch the waiter's attention.

GORDON: Waiter.

> *The unseen waiter ignores him. GORDON self-consciously lowers his arm and picks up his menu to hide his embarrassment.*

> *DYMPIE enters and surveys the scene as GORDON looks up from his menu and notices her. DYMPIE chooses her table. She walks to it, removes the ashtray and places it down elsewhere. She places a handbag on a seat then sits. Once seated, she blows out the candle and arranges herself for maximum comfort. Satisfied, she now surveys the scene again and notices GORDON watching her. They both look quickly away, back to their menus.*

> *PAULA enters. She wears a bright, colourful dress with a hood attached which she wears over her head. This is in marked contrast to DYMPIE's more plain attire.*

DYMPIE: [*speaking across the room while trying not to attract attention to herself*] Paula …

> *GORDON looks at PAULA.*

DYMPIE: [*motioning for her to approach*] Paula …

PAULA: [*speaking across the room*] Why don't we sit a little closer tonight.

DYMPIE: No, I've got one here.

PAULA: Yes, but I thought we could sit a little closer.

DYMPIE: No, this is fine.

PAULA: But last week I couldn't see.

DYMPIE: Paula.

PAULA: Last week we couldn't see.

DYMPIE: Paula … come here.

PAULA *approaches the table.*

DYMPIE: If you want to say something to me then come here and say it. Don't stand on the other side of the room and shout at me. Look, you've attracted the attention of the entire bistro.

PAULA *looks at* GORDON *who quickly looks back at his menu. She then sits down checking her view of the dance floor.*

PAULA: There's still plenty of tables closer.

DYMPIE: They don't serve meals at those tables Paula. You know that.

PAULA: Perhaps if we asked somebody. Perhaps if we told them we can't see from here.

PAULA *swaps seats and checks the view.*

DYMPIE: You can go and sit there if you want. Go on. Monika and I will stay here. Who wants to sit that close to the bar anyway? I certainly don't.

PAULA *swaps back to the other chair.*

DYMPIE: Stop that. Stop that changing of chairs. Decide where you're going to sit and stay there.

PAULA *thinks about it then goes back to the other chair much to* DYMPIE*'s increasing frustration.* PAULA *takes a box of matches from her bag.*

PAULA: [*relighting candle*] One night I'd just like to sit closer to the band. Closer to the other people.

DYMPIE: And be suffocated by cigarette smoke and have alcohol poured all over you by drunken men. Lovely. That would be lovely, wouldn't it Paula? You'd like that wouldn't you? No thank you, not me. And besides I don't like standing all night. I can't see the point of it when there are all these tables back here. You might be able to Paula but it's beyond me … Are you going to sit there all night with that hood over your head? Is that the fashion now, is it? To walk around with a hood over your head.

PAULA *removes the hood.* DYMPIE *notices her make-up.*

DYMPIE: What have you done to your face?

PAULA: Nothing.

DYMPIE: You have. You've done something to your face.

PAULA: I've put a bit of colour on, that's all.

DYMPIE: A bit! ... It's lovely. Bit loud, but no, it's lovely. What, get it out of some magazine did you?

PAULA: No, just experimented.

DYMPIE: Experimented.

PAULA: I like a change.

DYMPIE: Oh I know that, Paula. You don't have to tell me. [*Pronouncing it 'sham-el-on'*] A regular chameleon you are.

PAULA: You should take to wearing a bit, Dymp. Just a touch around the eyes.

DYMPIE: I am wearing just a touch around the eyes.

PAULA: You should think about wearing just a touch more.

DYMPIE: No, I don't think so.

PAULA: You should think about it.

DYMPIE: No.

PAULA: You'd be surprised.

DYMPIE: Not me, Paula. You won't see me with my face painted like some silly little tart trying to look half her age. Sorry, but no, not me.

GORDON *notices the waiter again.*

GORDON: [*raising his hand*] Waiter.

DYMPIE *and* PAULA *look anxiously to see if the waiter attends him.* GORDON *is ignored again. He self-consciously lowers his arm and returns to looking at his menu.* DYMPIE *and* PAULA *turn back to their own affairs.*

DYMPIE: Did you get those stockings I asked for?

PAULA: Yes, only I wasn't sure what size.

DYMPIE: I told you what size.

PAULA: Did you?

DYMPIE: I told you.

PAULA: What size?

DYMPIE: Average.

PAULA: [*taking the stockings from her bag*] Well I got you small.

DYMPIE: Not now, Paula. Don't give them to me now.

PAULA: What do you want me to do with them then?

DYMPIE: Put them away. Give them to me later.

PAULA *puts the stockings back into her bag.*

DYMPIE: Why did you get me small when I told you average.

PAULA: I thought you could wear a smaller size.

DYMPIE: No, I wear average.

PAULA: Yes, but I thought you could wear something smaller.

DYMPIE: No.

PAULA: You need something tighter, Dympie.

DYMPIE: What?

PAULA: I've been meaning to say something to you for ages, but your stockings bunch around your ankles.

DYMPIE: They don't.

PAULA: Everyone notices as you walk around the office.

DYMPIE: Who notices?

PAULA: Everyone.

DYMPIE: [*pulling her stockings up under the table*] Paula, my stockings do not bunch around my ankles.

PAULA: And you should try another colour as well, like black.

DYMPIE: Black! But I only wear bone.

PAULA: They're old fashioned, Dymp. Men don't find them attractive.

DYMPIE: What would you know about what men find attractive?

PAULA: You should try something sheer.

DYMPIE: All that doesn't concern me.

PAULA: Black and sheer, that's what men find attractive.

DYMPIE: The sort of man that judges you on your stockings is not the sort of man I want to spend the rest of my life with, Paula.

PAULA: Anyway, I got you black.

DYMPIE: But I only wear bone. Average and bone.

PAULA: Oh well, they fit me, I'll wear them.

DYMPIE: You will not. You got those stockings for me. Now give them to me … give them to me.

> PAULA *hands over the stockings.* DYMPIE *snatches them and shoves them into her handbag.* GORDON *rises from his table and wanders over to a print hanging on the wall. He studies it as though he is in a gallery.* DYMPIE *and* PAULA *look at him then* DYMPIE *resumes the conversation while* PAULA *lingers on* GORDON.

DYMPIE: It must be past seven.

PAULA: What?

DYMPIE: Where is she? I told her seven o'clock.

PAULA: Maybe she's not coming.

DYMPIE: Of course she's coming.

PAULA: Maybe she's not up to it.

DYMPIE: She promised she would. I made her promise.

PAULA: Maybe she's decided she doesn't want company after all.

DYMPIE: Would you stop it. You're a prophet of doom, that's all you are Paula.

PAULA: She's still not over it.

DYMPIE: I told her it would be good for her. Get out of the house. Have some fun. I told her that.

PAULA: Terrible thing.

DYMPIE: Yes.

PAULA: It wasn't expected.

DYMPIE: You don't have to tell me. You forget. My desk is right next to hers. She tells me a lot more than she tells you. Your desk is way over on the other side of the office.

PAULA: I found her having a little cry in the toilets.

DYMPIE: So did I. Several times.

PAULA: Poor thing.

DYMPIE: Yes, well, she'll get over it.

PAULA: I hope so.

DYMPIE: It would be best if nothing was said tonight.

PAULA: About what?

DYMPIE: The husband Paula. The husband.

PAULA: What if she wants to talk about it?

DYMPIE: Best just to avoid it.

PAULA: I'm not sure about that Dymp.

DYMPIE: I am.

PAULA: She might have feelings she needs to express.

DYMPIE: No, I think it would be better just to avoid the whole subject. Just carry on as though nothing's happened.

> MONIKA *enters, but remains standing on the other side of the room looking a little anxious. She has obviously made an effort and dressed for the occasion.* PAULA *sees her.*

PAULA: There she is.

> GORDON *is caught between* DYMPIE *and* PAULA's *table and* MONIKA. *He awkwardly gets out of the way.*

DYMPIE: What's the matter with her Paula?

PAULA: She's alright.

DYMPIE: Tell her to come over.

PAULA: [*across the room*] Monika ... youwhooo, over here.

DYMPIE: What's she doing?

PAULA: I don't know.

DYMPIE: Has she seen us?

PAULA: Yes, look she's waving.

DYMPIE: But she should come over Paula. [*waving back*] Why is she waving at us like that?

PAULA: It's alright Dymp, she's coming.

> MONIKA *approaches the table.* PAULA *stands to greet her.*

MONIKA: [*arriving at the table*] Here I am.

PAULA: Here she is.

MONIKA: I was just looking.

DYMPIE: Yes.

PAULA: What at?

DYMPIE: Paula! ... Hello Monika.

MONIKA: Hello Dymp.

DYMPIE: Sit down.

PAULA: Yes, sit down, sit down.

MONIKA: Where? Here?

DYMPIE: Anywhere.

MONIKA: I was just looking at it all. Taking it all in. Thinking I'm actually here. As little as a week ago I thought I'd never be able to do this sort of thing again. I couldn't even face going out of the house. And now ... well, here I am.

DYMPIE: Yes.

PAULA: Here you are.

DYMPIE: So sit down.

MONIKA: I hope I'm not too late. I'm not too late am I?

DYMPIE: No.

PAULA: We were just beginning to wonder where you were.

DYMPIE: No we weren't.

MONIKA: It took me so long to get ready. There I was just out of the shower when it occurred to me that I'd forgotten what I was meant to do first, my hair or my nails. And of course I couldn't decide what to wear.

PAULA: You look lovely.

MONIKA: So I just put on this old thing. It didn't make me feel right, but oh well ...

PAULA: No, it's lovely.

DYMPIE: Lovely.

MONIKA: Then I couldn't think where I'd put my car keys.

PAULA: I'm always doing that, aren't I Dymp?

DYMPIE: Always.

MONIKA: And my street directory's got pages missing so I got lost on my way here.

DYMPIE: Well you're here now.

PAULA: Yes, you're here now.

DYMPIE: So sit down.

> MONIKA *sits down in* PAULA*'s seat.* PAULA *looks momentarily panicked as she realises she's lost the best view of the dance floor. But she accepts the situation and sits in the other seat.*

MONIKA: It's been so long since I've been out. I mean I've been out but it's been so long since I've been out like this ... like ...

PAULA: On your own.

DYMPIE: Paula!

MONIKA: Yes, that's it. On my own.

DYMPIE: Well you're here now.

MONIKA: I've always been driven.

DYMPIE: And you look lovely.

MONIKA: Martin always drove.

PAULA: Lovely.

MONIKA: Silly really.

PAULA: A little tired though.

DYMPIE: Don't be ridiculous Paula. Monika doesn't look tired.

PAULA: No, just a little.

DYMPIE: Monika looks the best she's looked for a long time. Your make-up, lovely ... lovely.

PAULA *and* DYMPIE *exchange glances.*

DYMPIE: And you've lost weight. She's lost weight, hasn't she Paula?

PAULA: Since when?

MONIKA: I haven't really.

DYMPIE: Of course you have. Around the face. She's lost it around the face. Tell her she's lost it around the face Paula.

PAULA: You mean since we saw her at work this afternoon?

DYMPIE: No, of course not. Since before that. Since the last time ... you know what I mean. You know what I mean, don't you Monika?

MONIKA: [*not sure*] Ah ...

DYMPIE: Monika knows what I mean.

MONIKA: I'm hardly what you'd call thin, though. I'm certainly not as thin as Paula.

DYMPIE: No. But nobody is as thin as Paula. Paula eats like a horse and still looks like she's spent the last six months in a concentration camp. You know what they call her, don't you? They call her Belsen Paula.

PAULA: That's not very nice Dympie.

DYMPIE: She packs it away though.

PAULA: Not really.

DYMPIE: She does. I've seen her. She packs it away. Don't know how she does it. Probably goes home and vomits it all up.

PAULA: No.

DYMPIE: Gorges herself then sticks her finger down her throat.

PAULA: I don't. Monika, I don't.

MONIKA *laughs, not really sure whether she should.*

DYMPIE: Anorexia. That's her problem. She's anorexic.

PAULA: I'm not. Honestly. Besides, you're thinking of bulimia.

DYMPIE: Then you're bulimic. It all amounts to the same thing. You stuff it in then you can't wait to get it out.

MONIKA: [*looking around the bistro*] This is quite nice.

DYMPIE: You haven't been here before.

MONIKA: No.

DYMPIE: She hasn't been here before, Paula. We forgot. This is your first time.

MONIKA: Yes.

PAULA: Isn't that funny. Seems like you come with us every week.

DYMPIE: Paula and I come here all the time, don't we Paula?

PAULA: Every Friday night.

DYMPIE: Well not every Friday night. But often. No, it's alright. Bit of a night out. Something to do.

PAULA: Beats staying at home.

MONIKA: I don't mind staying at home.

DYMPIE: Nor do I Monika. Nor do I.

PAULA: But not every Friday night.

DYMPIE: No, not every Friday night Paula. Monika and I didn't say every Friday night. But some nights. Then now and again it's nice to come out, with the girls, girls night out. It's a bit of fun. We like it, don't we Paula?

PAULA: Yes.

MONIKA: I've always been a bit of a homebody myself. Martin … that's my husband … Martin was quite content to stay at home. Well he was too tired wasn't he? They're too tired to go out after work, aren't they?

PAULA: Are they?

MONIKA: There was nothing he enjoyed more than to curl up in his chair in front of the telly. I used to watch him, there in the chair, so happy with his lot and I'd think to myself 'I'm the luckiest woman in the world. I really am the luckiest woman in the world'.

DYMPIE: Yes well, best not to talk about it.

MONIKA: Silly really.

DYMPIE: When we go to the toilet we won't be able to go together.

PAULA: No.

MONIKA: Why not?

DYMPIE: In case somebody takes our table.

MONIKA: They're not likely to do that, are they?

DYMPIE: We don't know that.

PAULA: We could leave our bags. Then they would know it was taken.

DYMPIE: They might be stolen.

MONIKA: I don't think that's likely.

DYMPIE: Nevertheless.

PAULA: We'll take it in turns. Two can go at a time, but one should stay here.

MONIKA: I don't mind going by myself.

DYMPIE: Well nor do I Monika, but sometimes it's nice to go with someone else. Of course, when it's just Paula and me, we can't do that.

MONIKA: You two go first then.

DYMPIE: I don't need to yet.

PAULA: Nor do I.

DYMPIE: Monika?

MONIKA: Ah … no.

Pause.

PAULA: Actually Mon, we've got something to tell you.

DYMPIE: What?

PAULA: You know.

DYMPIE: No I don't. What?

PAULA: About Monika.

DYMPIE: What about her?

PAULA: About her being single again.

DYMPIE: Paula!

MONIKA: No, it's alright. After all, that's exactly what I am now. Single. I'll have to get used to saying that. Single.

PAULA: Yes, well now that you are …

MONIKA: I don't have a husband any more.

PAULA: No. And now that you don't, we thought …

MONIKA: Single.

PAULA: Yes … and we thought that you might like to join us.

DYMPIE: Yes, on a regular basis.

PAULA: On our nights out.

DYMPIE: It's a nice night out, really.

PAULA: Lovely.

DYMPIE: Dinner and then entertainment.

PAULA: You see there's all sorts of things you can do when you're single.

DYMPIE: All sorts of things.

MONIKA: Like what?

DYMPIE: [*Lost for words*] Well … like …

PAULA: Like this. Like coming out to dinner with your girlfriends.

DYMPIE: Exactly.

PAULA: So you never have to feel lonely.

DYMPIE: Never.

PAULA: So we thought that you might like to join us, Dympie and I that is, in doing some of those things.

MONIKA: Yes, I'd like that.

DYMPIE: Good, that's settled.

MONIKA: Thank you.

DYMPIE: Best to look forward.

MONIKA: You know you two are the closest friends I have now. You tend to lose your friends, once you're married, especially your girlfriends. Your friends become his friends. Not that Martin had any. He liked to keep to himself mostly. Anyway, I just wanted you to know how special you are to me.

DYMPIE: Whatever we do we only do because we care about you Monika.

PAULA: We've been a little worried about you.

DYMPIE: No we haven't … I mean we have but we knew you'd pull through.

MONIKA: Oh yes, I've pulled through.

DYMPIE: Of course you have.

PAULA: You're blossoming.

DYMPIE: Blossoming.

MONIKA: Blossoming, yes.

DYMPIE: You haven't bloomed yet but you will.

PAULA: You're a beautiful rose. Just at the moment, you're covered in aphids.

DYMPIE: I think Monika's got the idea now Paula.

PAULA: All you need is some tender care, for an old friendly gardener to come along and spray you a little.

DYMPIE: Yes, alright Paula.

MONIKA: No, I like that. I like that Paula. I'm a beautiful rose just waiting to be sprayed by an old friendly gardener. I like that image Paula. I might use that in one of my poems. That is, if you don't mind. If you're not planning to use it yourself.

PAULA: No, I'm not planning to use it.

MONIKA: I've been writing these poems, you see. To express my feelings. I've been going to a grieving workshop. It's run by a woman called Terri. She's lost two husbands so she knows a lot about it. We all write these poems and then read them aloud. It's part of the therapy. Terri swears by it. Some of them are quite beautiful … perhaps I've brought one. I could read it to you.

DYMPIE: Oh … we should order.

MONIKA: [*searching through her bag*] Oh … I don't seem to have one with me.

PAULA: [*disappointed*] Oh …

DYMPIE: [*relieved*] What a shame.

MONIKA: Never mind. You might be able to read them all soon. Terri's planning to have them published in a book called 'Death by Those Who Know'.

DYMPIE: We'll keep an eye out for it.

PAULA: Yes, I'll ask at my bookshop.

DYMPIE: Anyway, here we are.

MONIKA: Yes, here we are.

DYMPIE: You've come and we're going to have a lovely time.

MONIKA: Yes.

DYMPIE: We're going to forget all about that and just have a lovely time. We're going to have a lovely meal and then we're going to listen to the band.

MONIKA: Yes, I'm looking forward to the band. Paula told me all about it.

DYMPIE: But we have to eat first.

PAULA: They come on after dinner.

DYMPIE: You see we had to eat here, otherwise we wouldn't have got a table. And I don't like standing all night. Do you? I don't. You see these tables are only for those who come to eat here.

PAULA: There are tables closer but Dympie doesn't like sitting there.

DYMPIE: Gets a bit crowded later.

PAULA: She likes to sit back here.

DYMPIE: Well, you can hear yourself think, can't you? Paula would like to sit right up against the speakers if she could.

PAULA: I like to be close to the band.

DYMPIE: She'd like to be squashed in among all those other people. But no, not me, I like a bit of air.

PAULA: It's just that we can't see very well from back here.

DYMPIE: We'll be able to see as long as people don't stand in our way. They're not meant to Monika. They're meant to leave the area in front of us clear … But if you'd prefer to sit closer … well we could if you really wanted to.

PAULA: Where would you like to sit Monika?

MONIKA: [*not wanting to offend either of them*] Well, it doesn't really matter much to me. I don't mind either way.

PAULA: [*disappointed*] Oh.

MONIKA: I would like to see the band though.

DYMPIE: But we can't move. They don't serve meals there and I'm not going to starve all night.

PAULA: But …

DYMPIE: That's an unusual frock you're wearing Paula.

DYMPIE, MONIKA *and* GORDON *all look at* PAULA*'s frock.*

DYMPIE: Isn't that an unusual frock Monika?

MONIKA: Is it?

DYMPIE: It's got this attachment at the back. This sort of sack thing that covers her head. Put it on Paula. Show Monika.

PAULA: No.

DYMPIE: Go on, put it on. Show her the sack at the back.

MONIKA: I'd like to see it.

DYMPIE: There now. Monika wants to see it so you will have to put it on.

> PAULA *covers her head with the hood and shows it to its best advantage. Pause as* DYMPIE, MONIKA *and* GORDON *all look on in silence.*

DYMPIE: Isn't that the most unusual frock you've ever seen?

MONIKA: Yes, it is.

> PAULA *removes the hood.*

DYMPIE: We should order some wine.

MONIKA: Why not?

DYMPIE: Something sweet or something dry?

MONIKA: I don't really mind. Something dry? Paula?

PAULA: I'd like something dry.

DYMPIE: But not too dry.

MONIKA: No, not too dry … Is there a wine list?

DYMPIE: Wine list?

MONIKA: That we can choose from.

DYMPIE: Paula and I usually just have the carafe.

PAULA: But we could try a bottle if you wanted to.

MONIKA: No. I mean if you usually just have the carafe.

PAULA: Seeing how it's a special occasion.

MONIKA: No, honestly, the carafe's fine.

DYMPIE: It all tastes much the same anyway.

MONIKA: Yes.

DYMPIE: The carafe it is then.

> DYMPIE *and* PAULA *automatically go on the lookout for the waiter.*

MONIKA: I wouldn't really know the difference anyway. Oh, I mean I know there's white and there's red, but beyond that … well. Martin and I didn't drink much. We'd keep something in the house though, in case anyone ever visited. It wasn't that we were against it. It's just that we never saw the need for it. Martin and I were so happy. We never needed anything to stimulate us.

DYMPIE: Paula, catch that waiter.

PAULA: Where?

DYMPIE: There, by that pillar.

PAULA: Which pillar?

DYMPIE: There, on the left, quickly.

PAULA *and* GORDON *call for the waiter at the same time.*

PAULA: [*calls*] Waiter.

GORDON: [*calls*] Waiter.

PAULA *and* GORDON *look at each other and smile.*

DYMPIE: No, we've missed him.

MONIKA: We'll get him on his way back.

DYMPIE: No, we've missed him.

MONIKA: We'll get him on his way back to the bar.

DYMPIE: No, he's gone I tell you. You don't know these waiters. They'll do anything not to serve you. Anything …

DYMPIE *notices that* PAULA's *attention is still on Gordon.*

DYMPIE: Paula, what are you doing.

PAULA: Nothing.

DYMPIE: Well don't. I mean don't go drifting off like that. It's rude. Now who's ready to order. I'm starving.

DYMPIE *takes her menu and starts to study it in detail. The others follow suit.* STEPHEN *enters carrying a half-drunk glass of beer. He surveys the scene.* GORDON *spots him and tentatively waves.*

STEPHEN: You must be Gordon?

GORDON *stands to meet him.*

GORDON: Stephen?

They shake hands.

GORDON: Fine thank you.

STEPHEN: How are you?

GORDON: Ah … sorry. Yourself?

STEPHEN: What, Brendon not here yet?

GORDON: Ah … no.

STEPHEN: [*releasing* GORDON'*s hand as he checks his watch*] Said 7:30.

GORDON: [*checking his own watch*] Did he? Ah … well past that.

STEPHEN: I was running a bit late myself. What do you make it?

GORDON: Ah 7:45. Yes, 7:45 or 7:46.

STEPHEN: I'm 7:50.

GORDON: Are you?

STEPHEN: Expect I'm right.

GORDON: Yes, sure to be.

STEPHEN: Checked it before I left.

GORDON: Wise.

STEPHEN: By phone.

GORDON: I'm always a bit slow.

STEPHEN: Never leave the house without checking first.

GORDON: I should get a new one.

STEPHEN: Quartz?

GORDON: Ah … no.

STEPHEN: Get quartz.

GORDON: Yes, I will.

STEPHEN: No winding.

GORDON: Remarkable.

> STEPHEN *indicates the women with a sly look.* GORDON *looks over, not really sure why he's doing it.* DYMPIE *and* PAULA *who have been watching the men, look back to their menus.*

STEPHEN: Noticed them when I first came in.

GORDON: Oh yes.

STEPHEN: Perfect choice of table. And there's three of them.

GORDON: Actually …

STEPHEN: So, Brendon not here yet.

GORDON: No.

STEPHEN: What time did he tell you?

GORDON: About six I think.

STEPHEN: You haven't been waiting?

GORDON: No. Well, a little.

STEPHEN: No, that's careless.

GORDON: I was a bit late myself.

STEPHEN: Making you wait that long.

GORDON: It didn't matter. I've been admiring the … [*Indicating the prints on the wall.*]

STEPHEN: A half hour either side, nobody minds but two hours. No, that's careless.

GORDON: Well, a little I suppose.

STEPHEN: Still, that's Brendon.

GORDON: Yes, that's Brendon.

STEPHEN: You have to forgive him.

GORDON: Always doing things like that is Brendon.

STEPHEN: Is he?

GORDON: Well, not always.

STEPHEN: Never done it to me.

GORDON: There you are then.

STEPHEN: Ordered yet?

GORDON: [*picking up the menu*] Ah no, had a glance.

STEPHEN: We'll wait for Brendon, shall we?

GORDON: [*putting in back*] Yes, no, fine.

STEPHEN: Not a bad place this.

GORDON: Yes, I've just been admiring the …

STEPHEN: Never been here before?

GORDON: Haven't you?

STEPHEN: No, you.

GORDON: Ah, me.

STEPHEN: Come along with Brendon.

GORDON: No, never.

STEPHEN: No, me.

GORDON: Ah, you. Sorry, yes, I've got you now.

STEPHEN: Drinking?

GORDON: Who?

STEPHEN: You. CanI get you a drink?

GORDON: I've just been trying to catch the waiter's eye.

STEPHEN: Don't bother. I'll go to the bar.

GORDON: No, here, I'll go.

STEPHEN: No, no.

GORDON: Let me.

STEPHEN: I'll get the first.

GORDON: That's very kind of you.

STEPHEN: What is it?

GORDON: What's what?

STEPHEN: What are you drinking?

GORDON. Ah …

STEPHEN: What's that in your glass? Gin?

GORDON: This? No, this is water.

STEPHEN: Water! You've been sitting here drinking water for two hours? What, are you sick or something?

GORDON: No.

STEPHEN: On antibiotics?

GORDON: No, no, nothing like that.

STEPHEN: Brendon said you needed some loosening up.

GORDON: Did he? That Brendon.

STEPHEN: You can say that again.

GORDON: He's a joker.

STEPHEN: That Brendon.

GORDON: He's a one.

STEPHEN: A one with the women alright.

GORDON: So he tells me.

STEPHEN: You just watch him tonight. He'll be into those three over there, you just wait and see. He kills me that Brendon. He absolutely kills me. What's he got that we haven't. That's what I want to know. Not that I do too badly myself, but that Brendon, he's beyond belief. You just watch him.

GORDON: I will. I will.

STEPHEN: Still …

GORDON: Yes …

STEPHEN: What about that drink then? What about something a little stronger.

GORDON: Well …

STEPHEN: Can't hurt. Taxiing tonight?

GORDON: No, I've brought my car.

STEPHEN: Well, we'll have to watch you then, skippa.

GORDON: I beg yours.

STEPHEN: Skippa.

GORDON: Oh yes, I see, skippa. Actually Stephen, I'm actually not a drinker by nature.

STEPHEN: What, not at all?

GORDON: No.

STEPHEN: But one or two can't hurt.

GORDON: It tends to make me ill.

STEPHEN: Oh, I see, no, that's no good. Still, one or two can't hurt.

GORDON: Well, not one or two.

STEPHEN: What can I get you then? Brendon and I usually start with a beer, settle the nerves.

GORDON: A beer would be fine, thank you.

> STEPHEN *drains his glass.*

STEPHEN: Won't be long.

GORDON: Thank you.

> STEPHEN *glances at the women as he exits.*

GORDON: [*calling out at the exiting* STEPHEN.] Thank you Stephen.

> DYMPIE *and* PAULA *have continued to watch* GORDON *while* MONIKA *has been studying the menu.* GORDON *notices them.* DYMPIE *and* PAULA *look back to their menus.* GORDON *sits down.*

MONIKA: There's so much to choose from. I'll never be able to decide. Perhaps the chicken cacciatore?

DYMPIE: Ah, no, best not to. Paula had that once and was sick for a week.

PAULA: It's true.

MONIKA: Oh.

DYMPIE: Now, how should we do this?

PAULA: Can we have an entrée tonight Dymp?

DYMPIE: You can have an entrée, Paula. You don't have to ask me.

MONIKA: Perhaps to start with we could get one or two entrées to share.

DYMPIE: Share?

MONIKA: A plate of calamari or something. [*She reads from the menu.*] 'Squid rings dipped in batter and deep-fried in our own special way. Served on a bed of shredded lettuce with tartar sauce and chips.' Mmm. That sounds lovely. I've never eaten squid before.

DYMPIE: Can't eat seafood. Brings me out in a rash.

MONIKA: Oh … then, what about the …

DYMPIE: Can't share an avocado vinaigrette. Bit awkward.

MONIKA: Then what about the prosc … prosc …

DYMPIE: It's ham with rock melon. Don't like mixing my savouries with my sweets.

MONIKA: No.

DYMPIE: No, I think the best idea is that we each get what we want separately. Then there won't be any disappointments.

PAULA: I'm going to have the [*pronounced perfectly*] pâté de foie gras.

MONIKA: Where's that?

PAULA: In the entrée section.

DYMPIE: Have you been having Italian lessons Paula?

PAULA: No.

DYMPIE: I'm not going to have an entrée. Monika?

MONIKA: Well, I'm not that hungry, I suppose.

DYMPIE: You're the only one having an entrée Paula.

PAULA: Oh.

DYMPIE: It's just that it will hold everything up. You'll get your pâté first and they won't bring ours out until you've finished.

Pause as DYMPIE *holds out and* PAULA *relents.*

PAULA: Well I suppose I won't have one either.

DYMPIE: Are you sure?

PAULA: Plenty of other times.

DYMPIE: It's only a lot of chopped up duck's insides anyway. Should we have Greek salad?

MONIKA: The what?

DYMPIE: The Greek.

MONIKA: Where?

DYMPIE: Salad Monika. Salad. Mind on the job.

PAULA: Does that come with lettuce?

DYMPIE: Or should we have the Thai?

PAULA: Does that come with lettuce?

DYMPIE: I think they both would, don't you?

PAULA: They don't always you know Dymp.

DYMPIE: Of course they do. A salad's a salad. It has lettuce. That's what makes it a salad, Paula.

PAULA: Not necessarily Dymp. Sometimes they have other greens like rocket.

DYMPIE: Like what?

PAULA: Rocket.

DYMPIE: Well rocket's just a fancy name for lettuce.

PAULA: Not really Dymp.

DYMPIE: Paula, I can't believe you're being so argumentative. Rocket is lettuce, isn't it Monika?

MONIKA: What?

DYMPIE: Rocket.

MONIKA: Where?

DYMPIE: No … The salads.

MONIKA: Whatever you say, Dympie. I'm not very hungry.

MONIKA *has become strangely preoccupied.*

PAULA: There's that waiter, Dymp.

DYMPIE: Quickly Paula, get him.

PAULA: Waiter.

DYMPIE: Louder.

PAULA: Waiter.

DYMPIE: Waiter.

PAULA: Waiter.

DYMPIE: Quickly Monika.

MONIKA: Waiter.

DYMPIE: No. Decide on your main.

MONIKA: [*starting to panic*] My what?

DYMPIE: Your main Monika. Your main.

MONIKA: I thought we were just having salads.

PAULA: Waiter. No, we're losing him.

DYMPIE: Quickly.

PAULA: No, he's gone.

DYMPIE: See what you've done?

MONIKA: I'm sorry.

DYMPIE: He knew we weren't ready. He could tell.

MONIKA: [*starting to sob*] I'm sorry.

DYMPIE: No, it wasn't your fault.

MONIKA: I wasn't quick enough.

DYMPIE: It was Paula's fault.

PAULA: Mine?

MONIKA: I'm sorry.

DYMPIE: You're too slow Paula. You're too slow.

MONIKA: I'm sorry Martin.

DYMPIE: No, it's alright, Monika. We weren't quick enough. That's all. It was nobody's fault.

MONIKA *has begun to make choking noises.*

PAULA: Monika?

DYMPIE: What's the matter with her Paula?

PAULA: It's all that pent-up emotion Dymp. She's pented it up for ages.

DYMPIE: Not now Monika. Now come on. Pull yourself together.

PAULA: Have a little cry Monika. It's alright.

DYMPIE: Is anybody watching?

GORDON *looks back at his menu.*

PAULA: She'll be alright.

DYMPIE: Quick, take her to the toilets.

GORDON *looks back at the commotion.*

PAULA: She's just having a little cry. Nothing to be ashamed of.

MONIKA *is finding it hard to breathe.*

DYMPIE: She's going hysterical.

PAULA: Monika … Monika, can you hear me?

DYMPIE: Of course she can't hear you. She's hysterical.

PAULA: It's Paula here, Monika. Can you hear me?

DYMPIE: Do something Paula.

GORDON: Could I be of any help?

DYMPIE: No.

PAULA: No thank you. It's just our friend.

DYMPIE: [*panicking*] Paula.

PAULA: She's had a little upset.

DYMPIE: Do something.

PAULA: Thank you for offering though.

GORDON: No, please, if there's anything I can do.

DYMPIE: [*snaps*] No.

> GORDON *sits back in his chair.*

DYMPIE: Slap her Paula.

PAULA: What?

DYMPIE: Slap her.

PAULA: No, I can't.

DYMPIE: Slap her.

PAULA: No.

> DYMPIE *slaps* PAULA. MONIKA *immediately calms down.* PAULA *is in shock.*

MONIKA: I think I'm alright now, thank you.

PAULA: You hit me.

DYMPIE: I know.

PAULA: You hit me.

DYMPIE: But I didn't mean to.

MONIKA: I'm feeling much better now, thank you.

PAULA: You hit me Dympie.

DYMPIE: But I meant to hit her.

PAULA: You've never hit me before.

DYMPIE: I know. I'm sorry Paula. I'm so sorry.

MONIKA: I'm fine now. Honestly. Just pretend that nothing happened.

It's just that for a moment I thought that Martin was still with me and I panicked. Isn't that silly?

DYMPIE: Yes.

MONIKA: I was thinking about what I was going to order when I remembered that I hadn't left anything out for Martin. I thought of him searching through the fridge and not finding a morsel. I wanted to say something, to tell you he'd be looking for his dinner but I couldn't get it out. It was as though a large piece of phlegm had lodged in my throat and my words couldn't pass it. But then I remembered. Martin wouldn't be wanting his dinner because Martin's not with me any more. Martin's dead. And the phlegm just slid away.

DYMPIE: Are you going to have the veal again Paula?

MONIKA: Poor Martin. If only I was a little quicker. To have held him in my arms before he went. But how was I to know? How was I to know he was about to die. Men don't have strokes when they're thirty eight years old. It wasn't my fault. It wasn't my fault, was it?

PAULA: No, of course not.

MONIKA: Have I told you how Martin died?

DYMPIE: Not the details, no.

MONIKA: We'd finished our dinner. Martin was in the loungeroom watching television and I was in the kitchen doing the washing-up. I'd nearly finished the pots when I smelt this most vile smell. So I put the dog outside but the smell didn't go away. I searched high and low through that kitchen. Martin couldn't stand unidentified smells. Then I realised that the smell was coming from the loungeroom. I went in and there was Martin sitting bolt upright in his chair with his nostrils quivering and the most terrible look on his face. He would hate me for telling you but he'd lost control of his bowels. Something he normally never would have done. 'Martin', I said. 'Is everything alright? 'No dear'. And they were his last words. He closed his eyes and slid off the chair. The poor man, he was such a clean person when he was alive. So sad that he had to die in such shame. And thank God we didn't have any children. And God knows we tried. Still, where would I be now if we had children? Not here, not out on the town having such a good time.

The three women and GORDON *sit in a mournful silence until* PAULA *brightens in a brave attempt to rescue things.*

PAULA: We should get up and dance.

DYMPIE: I don't think so.

PAULA: We should.

DYMPIE: Nobody else is.

PAULA: We could start it.

DYMPIE: I'm not getting up there.

PAULA: Monika?

DYMPIE: Monika doesn't want to.

PAULA: Yes she does. Don't you Monika?

DYMPIE: Paula, Monika does not want to dance.

PAULA: Why not?

DYMPIE: She doesn't want to get up there and make a fool of herself in front of all those people. But obviously you do, so go on, get up and dance.

PAULA: Not by myself.

DYMPIE: Why not? You want to, don't you?

PAULA: But not by myself.

DYMPIE: You're always going on about it. Week after week pestering me to dance with you. Hoping some man will come up and ask you. So go on, get up and dance.

PAULA: Everybody will laugh at me.

DYMPIE: Put your hood over your head. Then you won't hear them. It will be like dancing in a world all of your own.

MONIKA: [*standing*] Excuse me. I think I'll just go to the toilet.

DYMPIE: Go with her Paula.

MONIKA: No, I'd rather go by myself.

DYMPIE: But we haven't ordered yet.

MONIKA: I won't be long.

        MONIKA *exits.*

DYMPIE: I knew we shouldn't have asked her.

PAULA: She's lost.

DYMPIE: I'll never forgive her. Never.

GORDON: [*standing*] Ah ... excuse me. I couldn't help overhearing but will she be alright? Your friend? Is there perhaps something I could do.

DYMPIE: No.

GORDON: Ah.

DYMPIE: Everything is under control.

GORDON: Right then.

He sits.

PAULA: Thank you anyway.

GORDON: [*standing*] Not at all.

He sits.

PAULA: He's nice,

DYMPIE: He should mind his own business.

PAULA: You didn't have to be so rude.

DYMPIE: Why anybody thinks they have the right to hear anybody else's conversation in a restaurant is beyond me. Anyone who had any manners would ignore it. Especially when it's so personal ... where is she?

PAULA: She's just fixing herself up a bit.

DYMPIE: I'm starving Paula. I'm not going to sit here and starve to death while she cakes her face with make-up and resets that ridiculous hair of hers. I came here to eat. Not to listen to a detailed description of her husband's death.

DYMPIE *stands up.*

You stay here and don't let anyone near our table. And I mean that Paula. You're always letting someone take my chair. Always.

DYMPIE *exits.*

PAULA: [*speaking to* GORDON *at his table*] I'm sorry about my friend.

GORDON: [*standing*] No need to apologise.

PAULA: She's not always like that.

GORDON: I'm sure she's not. But you can forgive her under the circumstances, losing her husband like that.

PAULA: No, she didn't lose her husband.

GORDON: Didn't she?

PAULA: She's not married. The other one did.

GORDON: Oh … I thought it was the other one.

PAULA: Which one are you talking about?

GORDON: The one that went to the toilets.

PAULA: They both did.

GORDON: The one that went first.

PAULA: That's Monika.

GORDON: Ah.

PAULA: I was talking about Dympie.

GORDON: Ah, I see. I've got it now.

PAULA: And I'm Paula.

GORDON: Gordon.

PAULA: Pleased to meet you.

GORDON: Yes.

PAULA: Has your friend gone?

GORDON: No. At least I hope not. He's gone to the bar.

PAULA: Expect he'll come back.

GORDON: Yes, I'm sure he will.

PAULA: Just the two of you is there?

GORDON: Actually we're waiting for a mutual friend.

PAULA: So there'll be three of you then?

GORDON: Yes.

PAULA: Isn't that funny. There's three of us too.

GORDON: Yes.

He laughs nervously. A pause. GORDON *goes to sit down.*

PAULA: Come here often?

GORDON: [*standing*] No … first time.

PAULA: It's quite nice sometimes.

GORDON: Yes, I've just been admiring the print on the wall. I have one
    just like it at home. Matisse, I think. [*It's not.*]

PAULA: Oh … you're artistic.

GORDON: Well … not really.

PAULA: It can get quite bohemian here.

GORDON: I can imagine.

PAULA: Later.

GORDON: Later?

PAULA: After dinner, when the band starts.

GORDON: Ah yes, the band.

PAULA: Sometimes people dance.

GORDON: Not much of a dancer myself.

PAULA: You don't have to be very good.

GORDON: May as well have two left feet.

PAULA: I'm sure you're not that bad.

GORDON: I am I'm afraid.

DYMPIE *enters. She's wearing make-up remarkably similar to* PAULA'*s. She notices* GORDON *and* PAULA *have been talking.*

DYMPIE: [*approaching the table*] Paula.

PAULA: [*gets a start*] What?

GORDON *moves back to his own table and sits.* DYMPIE *sits down.*

DYMPIE: She won't have a bar of me.

PAULA: You've done something to your face.

DYMPIE: She might listen to you. Go and see if she's alright.

PAULA: You've copied my make-up.

DYMPIE: Paula, I haven't copied your make-up. I've put a touch on around the eyes, that's all. You suggested it. Now go and see if Monika's alright, would you.

PAULA *gets up and heads towards the toilets. She passes* GORDON'*s table on the way.*

PAULA: I'm not leaving.

GORDON: [*standing*] Oh.

PAULA: Just going to see if my friend's alright.

PAULA *exits.* GORDON *sits down.* DYMPIE *blows out the candle then looks over to* GORDON.

DYMPIE: I'm sorry about my friend. I hope she didn't bother you.

GORDON: [*standing*] Not at all.

DYMPIE: She can be a bit forward.

GORDON: It must have been a terrible loss.

DYMPIE: Beg yours?

GORDON: Losing her husband like that.

DYMPIE: No, not that one. The dark one.

GORDON: Oh Paula.

DYMPIE: Introduce herself, did she?

GORDON: Yes.

DYMPIE: I'm Dymphna.

GORDON: Pardon?

DYMPIE: My name is Dymphna.

GORDON: Yes, she mentioned …

DYMPIE: Did she? What did she say?

GORDON: Nothing.

DYMPIE: No, what did she say about me?

GORDON: She said you weren't married.

DYMPIE: So, nor is she. Funny thing to be talking about really, who's married and who's not. Are you?

GORDON: I was.

DYMPIE: Really.

STEPHEN *enters with the drinks.*

STEPHEN: Here we are Gordon. Sorry about that.

GORDON: Don't look now but there's been a bit of trouble.

STEPHEN: Trouble?

GORDON: An incident at the next table.

STEPHEN *goes to look.*

Don't look. It's all over bar the shouting.

STEPHEN: Been a fight has there?

GORDON: She's hit one of them and the other one's run off to the toilet.

STEPHEN: Hit her!

GORDON: Been a tragedy of late. Lost her husband.

STEPHEN: Really.

GORDON: Dreadful business.

STEPHEN: Still, explains the outburst though.

GORDON: Exactly what I tried to say to them, Stephen.

STEPHEN: What, you've spoken to them?

GORDON: I offered my assistance, yes.

STEPHEN: You sly devil.

GORDON: What?

STEPHEN: Moving in on them the moment you detected a vulnerability.

GORDON: It wasn't quite like that Stephen.

STEPHEN: Wait until I tell Brendon. He'll never believe we've set something up without him.

GORDON: I do think you've misunderstood.

STEPHEN: Here's cheers Gordon. Here's to the dangerous night ahead of us.

STEPHEN drinks, *GORDON* sips.

STEPHEN: I might just pop over and introduce myself as well.

GORDON: Ah …

STEPHEN approaches *DYMPIE*'s *table*.

But Stephen …

STEPHEN: Hello … I just wanted to come over and say how sorry I was to hear about your husband. It must have been a terrible shock. What, about your age was he, early twenties? My name is Stephen, by the way. I'm just over at that table. If you need anything, I'm just a wave away.

STEPHEN backs away leaving *DYMPIE* wondering whether she should be insulted or flattered.

She'll be alright. Still in a bit of shock I think. Soon as Brendon gets here, we'll fill up on a few of these and move in on them.

GORDON: I'm not very good at that sort of thing, Stephen.

STEPHEN: You've got to take a risk, Gordon. You have to approach a woman believing that she wants you as much as you want her. As soon as you doubt it she will doubt your ability as a lover. And as Brendon says, that's what they want Gordon. They want a man who's good in the sack. Women have changed. They won't waste time with fumblers any more.

GORDON: No, I think there's been a misunderstanding between us, that's all.

STEPHEN: A misunderstanding.

GORDON: You see, I didn't come here looking for a woman.

STEPHEN: But Brendon said your wife left you and that you needed a good night out.

GORDON: Well, yes I do but not with a woman Stephen. That's the last thing I need.

STEPHEN: But the plan was to bring you here and fix you up with a woman.

GORDON: I'm sorry. I had no idea they were your intentions.

STEPHEN: What exactly did you think our intentions were?

GORDON: I thought we might just talk.

STEPHEN: Talk!

GORDON: Yes.

STEPHEN: What, all night?

GORDON: Yes, well over dinner.

STEPHEN: And after dinner?

GORDON: Well, yes, then too. You see I haven't had the chance to talk about it with anyone yet. When Brendon was kind enough to ask me to join you for dinner, I became quite excited. The thought of spending an evening with two of my fellow men excited me.

STEPHEN: Excited you?

GORDON: Yes, you see I don't think I've been out with just men since I was a teenager. I've been looking forward to it all week. I thought that if anyone could possibly understand how I felt then it would be another man. The separation hasn't been easy for me. I've been a little battered by the whole thing. We had to sell the house of course and I've been living in a small flat ever since. I've isolated myself from the world, so to speak, but then again I had to Stephen, I had to. After all the bitterness, the disappointments and rejection, there's only one thing left to come back to, Stephen. Yourself. Only the very sad thing, the pitiful thing is that there's no guarantee you'll like what you find, when you get there. Can you understand that Stephen?

STEPHEN: No.

GORDON: I don't like myself very much. When your wife leaves you and makes you feel like you're not worth the ground she walks on, then you're not left with a very high opinion of yourself. And you need to talk to someone. You need to tell someone you've been crushed. You need to shout before you go mad, before you hurt someone or before you hurt yourself.

STEPHEN: Yes, alright Gordon.

GORDON: That's why I've come here tonight Stephen. I need to shout. I need to tell someone. But not just anyone. Certainly not a woman. I need to tell a man. I need the support of my fellow man.

STEPHEN: Maybe you should save this until Brendon comes.

GORDON: Men do have emotions Stephen. And they can express them if only they're allowed to. Believe me, a day has not passed since she left, that I haven't wept like a lost child. Collapsed on the floor in a heap of uncontrollable tears ...

STEPHEN: Shut up. Just shut up would you!

GORDON: I'm sorry.

STEPHEN: It's alright.

GORDON: No, I'm sorry.

STEPHEN: It's not your fault.

GORDON: I've made a scene.

STEPHEN: I'm sorry if you thought that Brendon and I were like that. I've got nothing against homosexuals.

GORDON: What!

STEPHEN: I just don't want to spend any time with one. Especially not my Friday nights.

GORDON: Don't misunderstand me. I'm not a homosexual. I only wanted to talk.

STEPHEN: But I didn't come here to talk. Brendon didn't say anything about talking or crying. I came here to chase a bit of skirt and to have a good time. I didn't come here to talk and express my emotions with my fellow men.

GORDON: Yes, I'm sorry. My mistake.

STEPHEN *and* GORDON *reach an awkward silence.* DYMPIE *has been catching snippets of their conversation.* PAULA *comes dashing in.*

PAULA: Quickly Dymp!

DYMPIE: Quickly Paula! You'll never believe what I've just heard.

PAULA: Monika's locked herself in the toilet and she won't come out.

DYMPIE: That man's a homosexual.

PAULA: She's crying Dympie. She's screaming.

DYMPIE: Shut up Paula.

PAULA: I tried to talk to her, I tried to help but she won't listen.

DYMPIE: If she wants to spend the rest of the night in the toilet then that's her problem.

PAULA: But what if she does something?

DYMPIE: Don't be stupid.

PAULA: What if she hurts herself?

DYMPIE: She wouldn't do it in a public lavatory, surely. She's just looking for attention.

PAULA: But what if she slashes her wrists or something?

DYMPIE: You'd like that wouldn't you Paula?

PAULA: We don't know what she's capable of in the state she's in.

DYMPIE: You'd like a little drama, wouldn't you?

PAULA: Perhaps we should call a waiter.

DYMPIE: If any waiter is to be called, then he will be called to take my order, not for any other reason.

PAULA: I should get back to her.

DYMPIE: And what am I meant to do? Starve to death listening to a homosexual talk about his feelings all night?

PAULA: What homosexual?

DYMPIE: Him. Him. The one that's been interfering with us all night. Didn't you hear what I said?

PAULA: He can't be.

DYMPIE: He is. His wife found out and left him.

PAULA: But he just can't be.

DYMPIE: Of course he can. There's no law against it is there? Is there? There should be.

PAULA: It's just not fair. They're all married or … that way.

DYMPIE: Oh, I see. Had your eye on him did you?

PAULA: No.

DYMPIE: Thought you might have a chance with that one, did you?

PAULA: I'd better check on Monika.

DYMPIE: Well you've missed out again.

PAULA: I better get back.

DYMPIE: I'll order without you.

PAULA: No, don't do that Dymp. You'll spoil it.

DYMPIE: Spoil it! Good God Paula it can't get much worse.

PAULA: Just give her a minute to fix herself up a bit.

DYMPIE: She'll need longer than a minute. That one'll need six months in a hospital before she's fixed up.

DYMPIE *buries her face in the menu.* PAULA *stares intently at* GORDON *as she exits.* GORDON *smiles but is a little put off by* PAULA*'s stare.*

STEPHEN: Funny this. Funny Brendon not turning up.

GORDON: We musn't be afraid of silences Stephen.

STEPHEN: First you want to talk, now you want to be silent. I'm not afraid of silence Gordon. You want to know about silence? I live by myself. You should be at my place on a Sunday night, then you'd know about silence.

GORDON: I'm sorry.

STEPHEN: Friday night is the only night I'm not silent. But if that's what you want then fine, let's be silent for the rest of the night, shall we?

GORDON: No.

STEPHEN: No?

GORDON: No, I want to talk.

STEPHEN: Then talk.

GORDON: Ah … [*Searching for a subject*] The bank.

STEPHEN: What?

GORDON: The bank.

STEPHEN: What about the bank?

GORDON: You work in the bank too. You were at Pascoe Vale. That's where you met Brendon. Expect you were sad to go.

STEPHEN: Not really.

GORDON: But surely you miss Pascoe Vale.

STEPHEN: A bit.

GORDON: I've only been there five months.

STEPHEN: They sent me to Templestowe.

GORDON: I've become quite attached to it though.

STEPHEN: I miss a drink after work with Brendon.

GORDON: After Jane left I threw myself into work.

STEPHEN: They're all married at Templestowe … or joggers.

GORDON: Things matter more to me now. Like helping the pensioners out with F.I.D.

STEPHEN: They all go straight home after work, to their wives and kids.

GORDON: I used to be of the opinion that if people were facing financial difficulty it was of their own doing. They shouldn't expect the bank to rescue them.

STEPHEN: Then at lunch time they're all getting into their togs and going off for a jog.

GORDON: I suppose that's one good thing that's come of all this. I'm more in touch with the tragic side of life now.

STEPHEN: Marriage isn't for me.

GORDON: I'm able to listen now, to hear what people are saying.

STEPHEN: I worked that out a long time ago.

GORDON: I wasn't capable of that before. I could be staring tragedy in the face and not even recognise it.

STEPHEN: No, marriage isn't for me.

> PAULA *comes dashing in.*

PAULA: She's gone.

DYMPIE: What?

PAULA: She's gone. I can't find her Dymp.

DYMPIE: But we haven't had dinner yet.

PAULA: What are we going to do?

DYMPIE: Perhaps it's all for the best.

PAULA: Phone the police?

DYMPIE: Two's company. Three's a crowd. I knew she wouldn't fit in. She's not really our type. No, best that she's gone. Sit down Paula.

PAULA: But …

DYMPIE: I've decided what I'm having. What about you?

PAULA: But Dymp …

DYMPIE: [*stern*] Sit down.

> PAULA *sits.* DYMPIE *shoves a menu at her.*

STEPHEN: It only ends up in divorce and then where are you? Left paying a big fat alimony.

GORDON: Doesn't apply in my case, I'm afraid. She was earning more than I was, much more.

STEPHEN: If a woman ever walked out on me, she wouldn't get a cent, no way.

GORDON: Jane and I started at the Commonwealth together. We were happy at the Commonwealth. And then she was snapped up by CHALLENGE. That's when all the trouble started. Onward and upward with THE CHALLENGE. What she always called her job suddenly became her career. The fridge was suddenly full of Chardonnay. And she was always wanting to go out. Always wanting to meet new people. But she knew I didn't drink. She knew that. In the end, she started going out without me. With her new friends from CHALLENGE. No, Jane wasn't satisfied. I could never satisfy Jane. It was such a shame because when I married her she was so content with what satisfied me.

STEPHEN: [*referring to his empty glass*] Well, that slid down.

GORDON: Oh, yes.

STEPHEN: Must have been thirsty.

GORDON: Look at that. Haven't even touched mine. You're getting away from me Stephen.

> GORDON *has another sip.*

My only regret is that we didn't have children. One or two little ones running about our feet. Something to share. If we had children she wouldn't have been off with her friends having cocktails. For the sake of the children she would have stayed, no matter how unhappy she was.

STEPHEN: Look, are you going to get another round or not? The usual practise is that you buy alternate rounds.

GORDON: Yes, yes, I'm sorry. So rude of me to let you sit there with an empty glass. I'll just finish this.

> GORDON *skulls his glass, managing to spill most of it down his front.*

Oh dear, look what I've done.

STEPHEN: Look, perhaps I better go.

GORDON: No, no. Wouldn't hear about it. My shout. Isn't that what you say? My shout.

STEPHEN: Yes, it's your shout.

GORDON: Right then. Won't be long …

> STEPHEN *heads for the toilets.*

Where are you going?

STEPHEN: To the toilet.

GORDON: You will come back, won't you?

STEPHEN: [*hesitates*] Yes, Gordon. I'll come back.

GORDON: Thank you … thank you Stephen.

> STEPHEN *exits one way,* GORDON *the other. On his way out he runs into* MONIKA *returning. She carries a glass of wine and is no longer precisely groomed. She wears no shoes, her make-up is smudged and her hair is in disarray.*

Oh …

MONIKA: [*hiccups*] Hello.

GORDON: Hello. How are you feeling now?

MONIKA: Wonderful. How are you feeling?

GORDON: Oh … very well thank you.

MONIKA: You've spilt something all over your tie.

GORDON: Yes.

MONIKA: [*searching her bag for a tissue*] It will stain.

GORDON: It's only beer.

MONIKA: [*wiping his tie*] You'll have to soak that when you get home.

GORDON: Yes I will. Thank you.

MONIKA: My husband used to spill things down his front. I was always having to soak his things. Still he's dead now.

GORDON: Yes, I'm terribly sorry.

MONIKA: See them. That's Dympie and Paula. They're my bestest friends in the whole world. Yoowhoo, Dympie, Paula.

> PAULA *tentatively waves.* DYMPIE *ignores her.*

Do you know what they call Dympie at the office? They call her Dumpie. Dumpie Dympie. Isn't that mean?

GORDON: Ah … yes.

MONIKA: It's so mean.

GORDON: I better get these drinks.

MONIKA: Drinks? You couldn't get me one, could you.

She drains her glass, gives it to GORDON.

Tell you what, better make it a carafe.

GORDON: A carafe?

MONIKA: I think Dumpie and Paula could do with a drink too, don't you? [*Fumbling in her purse*] Here, here, let me give you some money.

GORDON: No, no.

MONIKA: I insist.

GORDON: No, honestly, it would be my pleasure.

MONIKA: But I don't even know your name.

GORDON: Ah … Gordon.

MONIKA: Pleased to meet you Gordon. I'm Monika and this is my husband Martin.

She looks for him at her side.

Ah, no, he's not here.

She tries to give GORDON *some money but his hands are full.*

GORDON: Ah …

GORDON *goes to say something,* MONIKA *stuffs ten dollars in his mouth.*

MONIKA: There you are, Gordon. Can you manage?

GORDON *gives a muffled protest.*

Good.

MONIKA *moves back to the table as* GORDON *heads off to the bar.*

Here I am.

PAULA: Here she is.

DYMPIE: Oh, really. Where have you been Monika?

PAULA: We were worried about you.

DYMPIE: They close the kitchen soon.

PAULA: I thought you were lost.

DYMPIE: Where are your shoes?

MONIKA: I don't know … I've had an adventure.

DYMPIE: Oh yes?

MONIKA: I was in the toilet crying.

DYMPIE: Yes, we know that bit.

MONIKA: And all these faces kept peering over the door at me and they were the colour of rainbows. Blues, greens, yellows, pinks.

DYMPIE: What's she talking about Paula?

MONIKA: I couldn't stop crying and the more I cried the more rainbow faces would peer in at me. So I closed my eyes and was about to scream when I realised I already was. Then one of the women with the rainbow faces dropped these in my lap.

    MONIKA *holds out a packet of Valium.*

DYMPIE: [*taking them*] How many of these did you take, Monika?

MONIKA: I don't know. Enough to stop me screaming. And do you know, when I finally stopped I couldn't for the life of me remember why I was crying in the first place.

PAULA: Martin. You were crying about Martin.

MONIKA: No, no. I think I'd forgotten about him by then. When I got out of the toilets everything had changed. It was dark and the stars were flashing on and off. I was dying of thirst and there was this table full of drinks, so I started to drink them, all of them, until this woman slapped my face and pulled my hair. She chased me all through the dark place until I escaped through a door. But it was so bright I couldn't see. I kept stumbling into men.

PAULA: Men?

MONIKA: Men everywhere I turned.

DYMPIE: You were in the public bar Monika.

MONIKA: They were pushing me and catching me, twirling me around and around until I was sick on one of them. I must have fallen over or passed out or something because when I stood up, I was standing beside the coolest, greenest rock pool I had ever seen. And there were these beautiful, round, coloured fish swimming, up and back and into their holes.

DYMPIE: She's insane Paula.

PAULA: I think it's the drugs.

MONIKA: And and and at either end there were these men standing with fishing poles. I just had to get into that rock pool. I was so hot, I had to feel the water on my skin, so I took off my shoes.

PAULA: Your shoes!

MONIKA: That's where they are.

PAULA: Where?

MONIKA: Beside the rock pool.

PAULA: Oh.

MONIKA: So I climbed up onto the ledge and dived in ... but it was so shallow I hurt myself. Then I rolled over to float on my back and look at the sky but instead there was a circle of men's faces staring down at me. Laughing with yellow teeth, big fat red pockmarked faces, leering and breathing on me. Their hands like an octopus, all over me, smothering me. Then from nowhere two arms scooped me out of the rock pool and held me against the smoothest chest I had ever cuddled up to. With biceps like big potatoes and the squarest jaw bone, with just these tiny little prickles that brushed my cheek. And I kissed the reddest fullest lips and ran my hands through the thickest black hair. But the arms carried me back through the door, through the dark place where the woman chased me, back here, where I met another man called ... Gordon who's gone off to get us a drink.

PAULA: It all sounds so wonderful.

MONIKA: Parts of it were. Parts of it were a nightmare.

PAULA: Why doesn't anything like that ever happen to me?

> MONIKA *sits down. From the folds of her dress a pool ball falls to the ground and rolls across the floor. The three women stare at it.*

DYMPIE: What's that?

MONIKA: A fish.

> DYMPIE *and* PAULA *look at one another.*

DYMPIE: Well, now that you've returned from your little adventure, perhaps you'd like to re-join us. Though I doubt you'll find any green rock pools or biceps like potatoes here. No, there's only Paula and me here. Let's order shall we.

MONIKA: There's that waiter.

DYMPIE: Quickly, quickly, decide what you want.

MONIKA: Hasn't he got the sexiest bum you've ever seen? I wonder if they realise how flattering those tight black pants are.

DYMPIE: The veal Paula?

MONIKA: When was the last time you woke up with a tight little butt like that beside you?

DYMPIE: I think I'll have the T-Bone again.

MONIKA: Would you look at the curve of it? How do they make it stick out like that with nothing holding it up?

DYMPIE can't stop herself peeking.

PAULA: He's turning around Monika.

MONIKA: Have you ever seen such a flat stomach? Can you imagine how firm it must be.

PAULA: With just a tiny trace of black hair running down from his belly button.

MONIKA: And look, if you look lower you can make out the outline of his ...

DYMPIE: Stop it.

MONIKA: Can you imagine what's underneath those tight black pants.

PAULA: Leopard skins.

DYMPIE: Stop it Paula.

MONIKA: And underneath those?

DYMPIE: That's enough.

PAULA: It's only a bit of fun.

DYMPIE: I'm trying to think about what I want to eat.

MONIKA: So am I.

DYMPIE: Don't be revolting.

MONIKA: Martin's bottom was revolting. It certainly was nothing like that.

DYMPIE: Is there no way to stop you?

MONIKA: Martin's bottom was big and white and flabby. It was not the sort of bottom you wanted to cuddle up to at night. Martin used to pass wind in bed.

DYMPIE: Stop her Paula.

MONIKA: I've never heard anything like it. Like some great fog warning, it went on and on all through the night. Martin used to stain his underpants. Back and front. Yellow ones at the front and brown ones at the back. Do all men stain their underpants like that?

And who had to wash those underpants? I did. Neither of you have ever had to wash a man's dirty underpants, have you?

DYMPIE: No.

MONIKA: And you're probably never likely to either.

PAULA: No.

MONIKA: Do you want to know what it's like to be married?

DYMPIE: No.

PAULA: Yes.

MONIKA: Martin didn't like to do it that often. Sometimes several months would pass by before he would do anything more than peck me on the cheek. Not that I complained, mind you. But do you know how I knew when he wanted to do it? I'd be woken up in the morning by his disgusting little erection jabbing at my back. I'd lay there pretending to be asleep, hoping that Martin would go and do it to himself in the toilet. But once Martin wanted it there was no stopping him. He'd cuddle up to me and rub that thing up and down my spine, poking his tongue in my ear. The stench of his breath made me want to vomit. But instead I'd laugh and giggle, open my eyes with a smile and quickly turn on my back before he jabbed that worm into the first hole he could find.

DYMPIE: That's enough.

MONIKA: But there's more. Because once I was on my back Martin would straddle me, and from the fly of his pyjamas, his rubbed-raw, pointy, red penis would be staring at me, dribbling his vile semen all over my nightie. Oh yes, I tried to have children but I never could, because Martin could rarely wait long enough to get inside me. That man. That revolting, lazy oaf of a man. I saw him lying there in his own shit. And I refused to clean him up. I let his own mother come in and see him like that. I told her to clean up the shit.

DYMPIE: Is that it? Because I want to say something now. I'm sorry to have to say this but you give me no choice. I could accept a few tears and perhaps a little hysteria, given the circumstances. But Paula and I asked you to join us tonight out of the goodness of our hearts. We thought that you might appreciate the company. But instead of being grateful you have deliberately set out to ruin our evening. Now I'm not a narrow minded person. I can be as much fun as the next person. But I believe that given you have only so recently been widowed there is only so much fun you should have.

MONIKA: You think I've been having fun?

DYMPIE: As for all those tears you so liberally shed, hearing you describe in such unnecessary detail, the lurid and sick goings on of your bedroom, I can only question their sincerity.

MONIKA: Those tears weren't for Martin.

DYMPIE: You can be sure of one thing, we won't be asking you again.

MONIKA: Those tears were for me. I haven't been crying because I lost a husband. I've been crying because I didn't lose him sooner. For all those years wasted pretending I was happy. Wasted pleasing him, never myself.

DYMPIE: You've done a pretty good job of pleasing yourself tonight.

MONIKA: You bet I have. I made a decision in that toilet. From now on I'm going to please me. It's not too late. It's not too late is it Paula?

PAULA: No.

MONIKA: It's not too late. I'm a beautiful rose about to bloom. And watch out when I do because I'm going to … I'm going to find myself a man. Any man. I don't care. And I'm going to say to him 'Take me. Take me back to your place. I want to sleep with you. I want to sleep in your dirty filthy man's sheets.' But in the morning I'm going to wake up and leave while he's still asleep. I'm going to walk out and never see him again. I'm going to leave him there lying in his own filth … But right now, I want to dance. Paula?

PAULA: Yes, Monika?

MONIKA: Dance with me.

PAULA: Now?

MONIKA: Yes, now.

PAULA: But the band hasn't started.

MONIKA: I don't care.

> MONIKA *pulls* PAULA *up.* DYMPIE *grabs* PAULA's *other arm.* STEPHEN *enters.*

DYMPIE: Sit down Paula. You're not dancing.

MONIKA: Yes she is.

DYMPIE: No she's not.

They pull PAULA *as if they were playing tug-of-war.*

STEPHEN: Ah … I think you better let her go.

MONIKA: Come on, Paula.

DYMPIE: You're not going, Paula.

GORDON *enters carrying the drinks.*

GORDON: Oh …

DYMPIE *lets go, flying back into* GORDON. MONIKA *lets go, flying back into* STEPHEN. *They all end up on the floor except* PAULA *who's not quite sure which way to go.*

END OF ACT ONE

ACT TWO

Later that night. After dinner.

MONIKA, DYMPIE *and* PAULA *are at their table.* MONIKA *looks composed once again, with her shoes retrieved and back on her feet.* PAULA *has a dob of cream on her face, a leftover from dessert.* DYMPIE *is fixated on the dob of cream.* GORDON *sits at his table, alone, a half drunk bottle of wine on the table.*

DYMPIE *clears her throat, trying to catch* PAULA*'s attention.* PAULA *doesn't look but* MONIKA *and* GORDON *do.*

DYMPIE: Paula.

> PAULA *looks.* DYMPIE, MONIKA *and* GORDON *all wipe their cheeks with their serviettes.*

PAULA: Yes Dymp?

DYMPIE: Nothing Paula. Nothing.

MONIKA: What time is it?

DYMPIE: About nine.

MONIKA: What time does the music start?

DYMPIE: After dinner.

MONIKA: Yes, but what time after dinner?

DYMPIE: After dinner they start to tune their instruments.

MONIKA: But what time will they start playing?

DYMPIE: Twelve.

> *The three women and* GORDON *all sigh.* STEPHEN *swaggers in with two ports.* GORDON *stands to meet him.*

STEPHEN: Here we are, Gordon. I suppose you thought you'd lost me.

GORDON: No.

STEPHEN: Just paid a visit. Picked up a couple of ports on the way back.

GORDON: Ah …

STEPHEN: You do drink port, don't you?

GORDON: Well, I've come this far.

STEPHEN: You're only young once, that's what I always say.

GORDON: Me too. I always say that. You're only young once.

STEPHEN: [*indicating the women*] Tell me, been any further developments.

GORDON: Been relatively quiet, surprisingly.

STEPHEN: They hardly said a word over dinner.

GORDON: Yes, well, I suppose it's been a little awkward.

STEPHEN: Not like us though, regular chatterboxes over here.

GORDON: Yes.

STEPHEN: Tell you what, I might just go over and pay them a visit. You know, cheer them up. Can't have them looking so down in the dumps, can we? Not on a Friday night. Save that for Sunday I always say.

GORDON: [*as STEPHEN moves to the other table*] Me too, yes. Me too. Save that for Sunday.

> GORDON *sits.*

STEPHEN: Well, ladies, how are we feeling? Enjoy our meals did we? You seemed to from what I could see. Wolfed them down. Mind you so did I. I had the oysters. Wolfed them down. Wasn't sure if you noticed. Most expensive thing on the menu but why not? It's Friday night and you're only young once. [*Speaking across to* GORDON] Wasn't I just saying that Gordon? You're only young once.

GORDON: [*standing—thinking he's being asked to join them*] Oh yes, you're only young once.

STEPHEN: [*turning back to the women*] Did any of you have the oysters?

> GORDON *is stranded. He moves back to his table and sits.*

PAULA: No.

MONIKA: No.

DYMPIE: They bring me out in a rash.

STEPHEN: Ah, that's no good.

MONIKA: I had the chicken.

STEPHEN: Ah, the chicken.

DYMPIE: She left most of her vegetables.

MONIKA: The carrots. I left the carrots. They were cold. I ate the potatoes.

PAULA: I love potatoes.

DYMPIE: I had the steak.

STEPHEN: Rump?

DYMPIE: T-Bone.

PAULA: It was very big. Did you see how big it was?

DYMPIE: Big! It was all bone.

STEPHEN: They can be like that.

PAULA: I'm glad I had the veal then.

STEPHEN: Best to go for the rump.

PAULA: Crumbed veal it was.

STEPHEN: My mother makes that.

PAULA: Mostly crumbs.

DYMPIE: And for dessert?

PAULA: [*her favourite*] Strawberries and cream.

ALL: Yes.

> DYMPIE, MONIKA, STEPHEN *and* GORDON *all wipe their faces with their serviettes.* PAULA *doesn't catch on.*

STEPHEN: The band's due to start soon.

MONIKA: In three hours.

STEPHEN: You are staying for it?

PAULA: Oh yes.

DYMPIE: Of course we are.

MONIKA: No matter what.

STEPHEN: Might see you on the dance floor then.

MONIKA: You will.

DYMPIE: Perhaps.

MONIKA: I'll be there. I love dancing.

PAULA: So do I.

STEPHEN: Yes, well … best get back to old Gordon.

> STEPHEN *moves back to the table.*

GORDON: [*rising*] Everything alright over there? Sounded a little tense.

STEPHEN: No, no. It's all set up, don't worry. [*Sitting*] Now where were we?

GORDON: [*Sitting*] Jane.

STEPHEN: Were we? I thought we'd got past Jane.

GORDON: She wasn't satisfied.

STEPHEN: No.

GORDON: You know what I mean, don't you Stephen? I couldn't satisfy her. She wasn't very happy with our sexual relations.

STEPHEN: Really?

GORDON: I'm afraid not.

STEPHEN: Funny you should mention that. Sex.

GORDON: I must admit, it had become a little irregular.

STEPHEN: How irregular?

GORDON: Once a month. We liked to do it on Sunday afternoon but what with the garden needing so much attention and both of us working, it wasn't easy.

STEPHEN: Best to live in a flat, I always say.

GORDON: It wasn't that I was against it. Good heavens no. On our honeymoon, I think we did it three days in a row. But you wouldn't know about honeymoons, would you Stephen?

STEPHEN: No.

GORDON: No. But I did lose interest after a while. It wasn't that I no longer found her attractive because I did. Jane was lovely to look at. I just got tired of the actual doing of it.

STEPHEN: I never get tired of it.

GORDON: Bored I suppose.

STEPHEN: I'd do it all day if I got the chance.

GORDON: A cuddle, yes. I never got tired of a cuddle. A cuddle's lovely between a man and his wife but sex ... well, it doesn't hold all the answers, does it? Jane thought it did but it doesn't does it Stephen?

STEPHEN: Well ...

GORDON: You shouldn't expect it to hold all the answers. You'll only be disappointed ... but as I said, you have to remain philosophical about these things because in the end, all you have is yourself.

STEPHEN: Ah yes, that can be good too. Sometimes I do it five times a day. I know it's a little excessive but I can't help it.

GORDON: Help what Stephen?

STEPHEN: Mrs Palmer and her Five daughters.

GORDON: Who?

STEPHEN *indicates masturbation.*

Oh that. No, I never do it. Well occasionally but only since Jane left, mind you.

STEPHEN: I've never met anyone like you Gordon.

GORDON: Haven't you?

STEPHEN: When I first met you I thought you were a bit of a dickhead.

GORDON: Did you?

STEPHEN: But you're not a dickhead Gordon.

GORDON: Thank you.

STEPHEN: When you said you wanted to talk I wasn't sure how to react.

GORDON: I sensed that.

STEPHEN: I'm sorry about thinking you were a homosexual and all that.

GORDON: It's all forgotten.

STEPHEN: It's just that I've never met a man who talks about himself so seriously. But as I've listened to the way you talk about your feelings and all that … well, I've come to admire your honesty.

GORDON: Thank you Stephen.

STEPHEN: I only wish I could talk about myself in the same way.

GORDON: But this is your opportunity Stephen. Take it while you can.

STEPHEN: I want to.

GORDON: Do. I'm all ears.

STEPHEN: I don't know how to begin.

GORDON: Could I make a suggestion?

STEPHEN: Please.

GORDON: Just open your mouth and make a noise, any noise.

STEPHEN: Anything?

GORDON: Just let it come.

STEPHEN *opens his mouth.*

STEPHEN: No, I can't.

GORDON: Trust me.

STEPHEN *tries again. This time the most painful and distressing moan comes out. The three women look over.*

DYMPIE: My God, what's happening?

PAULA: It's the one that had the oysters.

MONIKA: He must have got a bad one or something.

GORDON: There, how does that feel?

STEPHEN: Better, I think.

GORDON: Then try this. Say the first word that comes into your head.

STEPHEN: Sex.

GORDON: Oh, that.

STEPHEN: Look at me Gordon. I'm a relatively attractive man, don't you think.

GORDON: Yes.

STEPHEN: You'd even describe me as handsome, wouldn't you?

GORDON: I think so.

STEPHEN: I have a regular job with a decent wage, not excessive but decent. I own my own car and I'm paying off a strata title.

GORDON: Are you?

STEPHEN: You'd say I'm a relatively appealing sort of man.

GORDON: Oh yes.

STEPHEN: Then can you tell me why I have never been able to maintain a relationship beyond the duration of a single night?

GORDON: Ah.

STEPHEN: I'm thirty-six years old Gordon.

GORDON: Are you?

STEPHEN: I probably don't look it, do I?

GORDON: No, thirty five at the most, I would have thought.

STEPHEN: The truth is that in all that time I've never had a girlfriend. One night stands, yes, plenty. But nothing more. And what I really want is that one night I'll leave here with a woman believing that this time it will be for longer, maybe even forever. I know I'm always saying that marriage isn't for me but it's a lie Gordon. That's exactly what I do want.

GORDON: I know.

STEPHEN: You do?

GORDON: I hope you don't mind me saying but I thought to myself earlier tonight, this man is desperately lonely.

STEPHEN: Yes.

GORDON: That underneath that bold exterior there's a sensitive man just longing to share that sensitivity with a woman.

STEPHEN: The thing is Gordon, I'm not very successful when it comes to women, either. Especially in the bedroom.

GORDON: Well, I can't help you there I'm afraid.

STEPHEN: It's all a mystery to me.

GORDON: It's a mystery to me too. Just ask Jane.

STEPHEN: I get so worked up about it all.

GORDON: I wish I could.

STEPHEN: I suffer from what the doctors call premature ejaculation.

GORDON: They've got clinics for that sort of thing.

STEPHEN: But it's not only that. You see, whenever I'm about to do it, I lose my erection.

GORDON: Well at least that solves the premature ejaculation.

STEPHEN: But it hardly makes for a satisfying sex life.

GORDON: No. Have you tried deep breathing?

STEPHEN: I've tried everything. I'm desperate Gordon.

GORDON: Yes, you must be.

STEPHEN: The only way I can stay erect … no, I can't. It's too embarrassing.

GORDON: No, go on, go on.

STEPHEN: The only way I can stay erect is to fantasise about other things.

GORDON: What things?

STEPHEN: I have to imagine that I'm a little boy … you promise you won't say anything to Brendon about this.

GORDON: My lips are sealed.

STEPHEN: I'm a little boy and I'm in a classroom. And the teacher, Mrs Haselmere, has kept me back after school for being naughty.

GORDON: Go on.

STEPHEN: And this Mrs Haselmere, she wants to play with my …

He indicates his penis.

GORDON: Really?

STEPHEN: It's the only way.

GORDON: [*remembering something unpleasant*] I had a teacher like Mrs Haselmere once.

STEPHEN: But if I think of Mrs Haselmere I never reach a climax. You see, in the fantasy Mrs Haselmere never gets to touch my …

He indicates his penis.

GORDON: Why not?

STEPHEN: Because just as she reaches into my pants my mother arrives to pick me up. So I have to go through the whole thing again and again and each time, just as I'm about to explode my mother comes in. Can you see my problem Gordon?

GORDON: Which one? There's so many.

STEPHEN: I'm a premature ejaculator. So I panic. Then I lose my erection. So to stop myself panicking I fantasise about Mrs Haselmere. But if I think about Mrs Haselmere I think about my mother. And if I think about my mother I don't come at all. I'm either coming too quickly or not coming at all. Gordon you've got to help me.

MONIKA: The carafe's empty.

They all look at the carafe.

Another?

DYMPIE: I couldn't drink a whole one by myself.

PAULA: No.

MONIKA: Well, neither of you will have to, seeing how there's three of us.

DYMPIE: But I only really want a glass.

PAULA: Just a sip.

MONIKA: The same?

PAULA: I enjoyed that.

DYMPIE: It wasn't too dry?

MONIKA: I didn't find it too dry. Paula?

PAULA: No, I didn't find it too dry.

DYMPIE: I did.

MONIKA: Something sweeter, then.

PAULA: But not too sweet.

DYMPIE: Paula, catch that waiter.

PAULA: Waiter.

DYMPIE: Again.

PAULA: Waiter.

DYMPIE: Again.

PAULA: Waiter.

MONIKA *stands up and yells.*

MONIKA: Waiter!

DYMPIE: Thank you Monika. But I think we've missed him again.

MONIKA *sits down.*

STEPHEN: Size is not the problem.

GORDON: Pardon?

STEPHEN: Penis size isn't the problem.

GORDON: No, well they say that, don't they. They say that women don't notice the difference. That they expand and contract to accommodate all sorts. But sometimes I wonder. Sometimes I wonder if Jane wouldn't have been a little happier if I was ... well, if I had a little extra down there.

STEPHEN: I'm sure that wasn't the case.

GORDON: She said as much before she left.

STEPHEN: She didn't!

GORDON: She did.

STEPHEN: That's low. No, that's really low.

GORDON: Yes.

STEPHEN: Well everybody else says it doesn't matter.

GORDON: Yes, everybody says that.

STEPHEN: But ... as long as we're being honest and if you don't mind me asking that is but just how small are you?

GORDON: Well, I wouldn't say small. No, I wouldn't say that. I'd say about ... average.

STEPHEN: But in centimetres, I mean.

GORDON: Ah, well, about [*indicating a length with his fingers*] so so.

STEPHEN: Ah, so that's about average, is it?

GORDON: More or less.

STEPHEN: I must be a little above average then.

GORDON: [*piqued*] Oh, are you?

STEPHEN: Just a little.

GORDON: I see.

STEPHEN: But as we were saying, size is not a problem.

GORDON: Well no, that proves it doesn't it? I mean if you are above average as you say you are and yet you still suffer from some of the most demoralising sexual disorders imaginable, then size can't matter very much, can it? I mean here I am, with a mere average one and yet I haven't suffered half the problems you have.

STEPHEN: No, you only have the one problem. You just don't like doing it.

GORDON: Not all the time, no.

STEPHEN: But most of the time.

GORDON: Best not to try at all than to try and continually fail.

STEPHEN: I think it's better to have tried and failed than never to try at all ... as humiliating as failure can be sometimes.

GORDON: Yes, you must have been dreadfully humiliated. You must have been humiliated so many times in your life Stephen.

MONIKA: Is that the bill?

DYMPIE *makes a grab for the bill.*

PAULA: How much?

DYMPIE: Now, how should we do this?

PAULA: More than last week?

DYMPIE: More. Much more.

DYMPIE *and* PAULA *look anxious.* MONIKA *takes twenty dollars from her purse and puts it on the table.*

MONIKA: Here's twenty.

DYMPIE: I don't think they've charged us for the salad.

PAULA: Wait, it's probably included in something else.

DYMPIE: No, they've made a mistake.

PAULA: Should we tell them?

DYMPIE: It wasn't that good really, the salad.

PAULA: No. It didn't have any lettuce.

DYMPIE: Then let's leave it shall we?

PAULA: What if they catch us?

DYMPIE: It's their mistake, Paula. It's not our fault.

PAULA: I'm not sure, Dympie.

DYMPIE: Let's?

PAULA: Alright.

DYMPIE: Now, how should we do this?

PAULA: Monika's put in twenty.

DYMPIE: We could third the total cost and each pay a third.

MONIKA: Why don't we just do that?

DYMPIE: Or we could each pay for our own main and split the cost of the carafe of wine and the garlic bread.

PAULA: Monika didn't get any garlic bread.

MONIKA: I think the band is about to start.

DYMPIE: Concentrate Monika. Then we can each pay for our own main, divide the cost of the carafe by three and halve the garlic bread.

PAULA: Actually Dymp, I didn't get any garlic bread either. You ate it all.

DYMPIE: No, I don't think you're quite right there.

PAULA: I don't mean to be picky but you did.

DYMPIE: Paula, I don't even like garlic bread.

PAULA: Well, it doesn't really matter, anyway.

DYMPIE: No, I think you've made a mistake, that's all, because I don't even like garlic bread.

PAULA: Well you did very well for someone who doesn't like it.

DYMPIE: I wish you'd wipe that cream off your face. It's difficult enough to have a serious conversation with you at the best of times. It's impossible when you've got cream on your face.

PAULA: What?

DYMPIE: You've got cream on your face Paula.

> PAULA *is horrified. She checks her face and wipes the cream away.*

PAULA: You could have told me.

DYMPIE: I tried.

PAULA: You could have discreetly pointed it out.

DYMPIE: Being discreet doesn't work with you, Paula.

GORDON: Is that the bill?

> *Both wait for the other to take it.* GORDON *takes it reluctantly.*

GORDON: Well, we may as well sort it out now.

STEPHEN: How much?

GORDON: A lot more than I think it should be given the quality of the service. I don't think we'll split the cost, if you don't mind, given that you had by far the most expensive things on the menu. I don't mind putting in something for the wine, but I'm not prepared to subsidise your oysters.

STEPHEN: But I paid for the ports.

GORDON: I didn't ask you to buy me a port. You did it entirely off your own bat.

> GORDON *fumbles through his wallet for the right cash and coin.*

Now, let me see, I think mine comes to seventeen dollars and sixty cents and yours ...

STEPHEN: Don't bother.

> STEPHEN *slaps his credit card on the table.*

GORDON: I couldn't.

STEPHEN: It's nothing.

GORDON: I insist on paying my own way.

STEPHEN: Don't make it awkward, Gordon. I want to pay.

GORDON: Then take the cash.

STEPHEN: Do you still use cash?

GORDON: I don't believe in plastic money. I never buy anything unless I can pay for it there and then.

STEPHEN: Honestly Gordon, you should update your thinking. If you want to get anywhere these days you can't afford to be running back and forth to the ATM. Frankly, with the company I keep, I'd be embarrassed to show anyone I still used cash.

GORDON: You and Jane should have got together. She was always going on at me about updating my thinking. She had credit cards, lots of them. More than you probably. Yes, you and Jane would have suited one another perfectly, with your credit cards and your larger than average member. But at least when I did make love to her it was her I was seeing and not Mrs Haselmere.

MONIKA: The band's starting.

DYMPIE: What?

PAULA: I can't see.

DYMPIE: They're not meant to.

PAULA: People are standing up.

DYMPIE: Somebody tell them they're not meant to.

PAULA: I knew this would happen.

DYMPIE: Call the manager.

MONIKA: Why don't we move?

DYMPIE: No. Paula, tell them to move out of the way.

PAULA: This is your fault. You make them get out of the way.

DYMPIE: [*speaking to the crowd*] Excuse me …

MONIKA: We're going to have to stand.

DYMPIE: No.

> MONIKA *and* PAULA *stand.*

Sit down. We don't have to stand. We had dinner here.

PAULA: You've done it again Dympie. Every Friday night you make us sit back here, as far away from anybody else as possible and we can never see.

DYMPIE: Paula.

PAULA: Just because you're too afraid to sit closer to the bar. What do you think is going to happen to you there? Are you frightened that some man is going to accidentally touch you.

DYMPIE: I've just about had enough of you Paula.

PAULA: Just once I'd like to choose where we sit.

DYMPIE: Shut up. Shut up you ridiculous silly woman.

PAULA: You say the cruellest things to me. I've given up counting the number of times you've hurt me. I don't know why I put up with it. I know you think I'm silly Dympie and you don't like the clothes I wear, even though you copy every thing I do. She copies every thing I do Monika.

DYMPIE: I do not.

PAULA: You wait and see. Next week she'll turn up with a dress with a hood on it and make out it was all her own idea.

DYMPIE: That will be the day. That will be the day you catch me with a hood over my head.

PAULA: But I don't let such little things bother me because I know that I'm an original person while you're just a copy cat.

DYMPIE: Copy cat!

PAULA: None of that really bothers me but I will never forgive you for letting me sit here for half the night with cream on my face.

DYMPIE: This is all her fault.

MONIKA: Mine?

DYMPIE: You and I have never had words before. She's come between us.

PAULA: It's got nothing to do with her. I've wanted to say this to you for a long time.

DYMPIE: We could move if you want. We could go and stand near the bar.

PAULA: Have you ever stopped to ask yourself why I have remained your friend?

DYMPIE: Don't Paula.

PAULA: There's not another woman at the office who can even bear to be in the same room as you. Do you know what they call you? Dumpie. They call you Dumpie Dympie. You're the plainest and loneliest woman I have ever known and I feel sorry for you. So you remember this, I'm the only friend you've got so the next time you see me with cream on my face, you tell me alright?

DYMPIE *is shattered by* PAULA*'s outburst.*

MONIKA: Ah … I think they've got a better view from their table. Why don't we join them?

PAULA: Yes, let's.

MONIKA: [*speaking across to the men*] Yoohoo! Gordon.

GORDON: [*from his table*] Hello.

MONIKA: Would you mind if we joined you? We can't see from here.

STEPHEN: No, please do. Bring your glasses and we can make a party of it.

PAULA *and* MONIKA *move over to the men's table, leaving* DYMPIE *by herself.* STEPHEN *and* GORDON *rise to join them. They all sit down leaving* GORDON *without a seat. He stands awkwardly among them.*

MONIKA: Oh yes, this is much better here. Look Paula, you can see clear through to the band.

GORDON: Isn't your friend coming?

PAULA: No, she can see perfectly from there.

> STEPHEN *fills the glasses but runs out before he gets to* GORDON'*s glass.*

STEPHEN: Sorry about that Gordon. Tell you what, why don't you run off to the bar and get us another before the band starts.

GORDON: Oh well …

STEPHEN: There's a good boy.

GORDON: Well, if the ladies would like something to drink.

BOTH: Yes please.

GORDON: Right then. Won't be long.

> GORDON *exits.*

MONIKA: I don't think we've met. Monika.

STEPHEN: [*taking her hand*] Pleased to meet you Monika.

> *They hold hands a little too long.* PAULA *notices.*

PAULA: They say that men who have dandruff shouldn't wear dark clothes.

> STEPHEN *lets go of* MONIKA'*s hand.*

STEPHEN: [*brushing his shoulder*] Oh God. I've tried to do something about it. There's nothing I can do. Can you suggest anything? I'll try anything.

PAULA: You'll just have to wait until you go bald. That will fix it.

> *The band starts with an up-tempo cover of 'The Boys Light Up'. They all look toward the band. As they listen, they start to move to the music, in their chairs.* DYMPIE *observes the others dancing in their chairs and does so herself.* GORDON *returns and seeing them bopping to the music, he turns and watches the band, moving self-consciously to the music. They loosen up as the song progresses. They keep this up until the end of the song.*

That was fun.

STEPHEN: Yes.

PAULA: I love dancing.

The next song begins, something slower—a cover of 'Lady in Red'. This sets a different mood between them. PAULA *looks hopefully to* STEPHEN.

MONIKA: Stephen, will you dance with me?

STEPHEN: Would I?

MONIKA *and* STEPHEN *get up and go to the dance floor.* GORDON *takes a seat.*

PAULA: I suppose you don't like dancing with women all that much.

GORDON: No, well I'm not very good at it.

PAULA: Have you ever done it?

GORDON: Once or twice.

PAULA: It must have been terrible for your wife.

GORDON: In what respect?

PAULA: Well, she didn't know did she?

GORDON: Oh yes, she knew even before we were married.

PAULA: But she still married you?

GORDON: It didn't seem to matter at the time.

PAULA: But she realised later that it did.

GORDON: It was part of it I suppose. Symbolic, in a way, of my inability to be free. I've always found it difficult to be open in public.

PAULA: It must have been terrible to keep it a secret for so long.

GORDON: Not really, no.

PAULA: But are you happy the way you are?

GORDON: I'm trying to accept what I am.

PAULA: But haven't you ever tried to change things? Gone to a doctor or something?

GORDON: I never thought it was that serious.

PAULA: Maybe your wife wasn't the right woman for you.

GORDON: She wasn't. I found that out the hard way.

PAULA: It's a lot safer now to do it with women.

GORDON: I don't follow.

PAULA: AIDS.

GORDON: AIDS?

PAULA: You're more likely to catch AIDS, aren't you? Being a homosexual?

GORDON: But I'm not a homosexual.

PAULA: Aren't you?

GORDON: No.

PAULA *scowls at* DYMPIE.

PAULA: I'm so sorry. Somebody told me you were.

GORDON: Everyone thinks I am tonight.

PAULA: How embarrassing.

GORDON: Maybe I am and I'm the only one who doesn't know it.

PAULA: I'm sure you're not.

GORDON: No, I don't think I am either.

PAULA: Does this mean you'll dance with me?

GORDON: Alright. If you don't mind having your toes trodden on.

PAULA: No, I don't mind. I don't mind at all.

They get up just as the song finishes.

GORDON: Oh.

PAULA: Oh.

They clap. The next song begins and they join STEPHEN *and* MONIKA *on the dance floor. This time it's 'Total Control'.* DYMPIE *sits alone and abandoned. She sways a little, trying to give the impression that she's having a good time.*

DYMPIE: [*speaking to the crowd in front of the table*] Excuse me. Excuse me, yes you. Would you mind sitting down? I can't see. These tables are for the people who came to eat here. We're meant to have an unobstructed view of the performing area. Now please … please …

She is ignored. Gathering her resolve, she stands. She still can't see. She stands up on the chair. Still unable to see clearly, she takes one step further and moves up onto the table. From here she looks out across a commanding view of the bar.

DYMPIE: I can see. I can see perfectly from here. I have a clear view right to the band. Paula … Paula? Did you hear that? [*Shouting.*] Paula!

The music cuts out. Everybody turns to look.

DYMPIE: I can see. I can see perfectly from here. And I'm the plainest and loneliest woman in the world.

A deathly silence. DYMPIE *returns from her moment of triumph and realises she has attracted the attention of the entire bistro.*

She gets down from the table and resumes her seat. A slow number begins. MONIKA *and* STEPHEN *resume their dancing. From the dance floor* PAULA *looks sadly at her friend.*

PAULA: Gordon, would you do something for me?

GORDON: Anything.

PAULA: Would you go and ask Dympie to dance? I know she can be a bit rude but she's harmless really.

GORDON: What about you?

PAULA: I'll be alright.

GORDON: Are you sure?

> PAULA *nods.* GORDON *approaches* DYMPIE.

GORDON: Excuse me.

DYMPIE: What do you want?

GORDON: Would you like to dance?

DYMPIE: Did Paula put you up to this?

GORDON: Ah … she suggested it, yes.

DYMPIE: Is this another one of her tricks?

GORDON: No, no, I assure you.

DYMPIE: She's a funny one that Paula. But she's alright really, underneath it all. I don't know what she'd do without me.

GORDON: Yes, I'm sure.

DYMPIE: I'll dance with you on one condition.

GORDON: Anything.

DYMPIE: You don't get any saliva on me.

GORDON: Oh … no, well I'll try not to.

> DYMPIE *and* GORDON *move onto the dance floor.* PAULA *looks on and puts her hood over her head and begins to dance by herself.*

MONIKA: Stephen?

STEPHEN: Mmm?

MONIKA: Are your sheets dirty?

STEPHEN: No. I mean they are but I've got clean ones in the cupboard.

MONIKA: [*disappointed*] Oh.

STEPHEN: I could always get some dirtier ones out of the laundry basket, if you like.

MONIKA: Would you?

STEPHEN: Are you into dirty sheets?

MONIKA: Tonight I am, yes … if you're willing.

STEPHEN: Yes, I'm willing but there's something I want to talk to you about first.

MONIKA: Tell me tomorrow Stephen. When you wake up. Save it till then. Let's go shall we … ?

She collects her things and then passes DYMPIE *and* GORDON *on her way out.*

MONIKA: Goodbye Dympie.

DYMPIE: You're going are you?

MONIKA: Yes, thank you for a lovely evening.

DYMPIE: I'm glad you had a good time. We'll see you in the office on Monday.

MONIKA: Yes … at least I think so. Goodbye Paula.

DYMPIE: She won't hear you. She's in a world of her own, that one.

MONIKA: Say goodbye for me.

STEPHEN: I'll see you later then Gordon. Don't do anything I wouldn't.

GORDON: No I won't.

STEPHEN: You'll see Brendon on Monday, won't you?

GORDON: Yes.

STEPHEN: [*indicating* MONIKA] You'll fill him in then, what he missed out on.

GORDON: Yes.

STEPHEN *and* MONIKA *move away.*

GORDON: Stephen …

STEPHEN *looks back.*

GORDON: Give my regards to Mrs Hazelmere.

STEPHEN *and* MONIKA *exit.* DYMPIE *and* GORDON *resume dancing.* PAULA *continues to dance in a world of her own.* GORDON *looks over to* PAULA *as* DYMPIE *moves in and lays her head on* GORDON*'s shoulder. The lights fade.*

THE END